Apr 2016

BUFFALO BILLS

BY BARRY WILNER

The Child's World®

Published by The Child's World®
1980 Lookout Drive • Mankato, MN 56003-1705
800-599-READ • www.childsworld.com

Acknowledgments
The Child's World®: Mary Berendes, Publishing Director
Red Line Editorial: Editorial direction
The Design Lab: Design
Amnet: Production

Design Element: Dean Bertoncelj/Shutterstock Images
Photographs ©: Evan Pinkus/AP Images, cover; Kevin
Terrell/AP Images, 5; Bill Wippert/AP Images, 7, 21; Gary
Wiepert/AP Images, 9; Alan Diaz/AP Images, 11; Richard
Cavalleri/Shutterstock Images, 13; David Drapkin/AP
Images, 14-15; Bill Sikes/AP Images, 17; Susan Ragan/AP
Images, 19; NFL/AP Images, 23; Nam Y. Huh/AP Images,
25; Kathy Willens/AP Images, 27; Kevin Higley/AP
Images, 29

ISBN 9781631439872
LCCN 2014959657

Printed in the United States of America
Mankato, MN
July, 2015
PA02265

ABOUT THE AUTHOR

Barry Wilner has written more than 40 books, including many for young readers. He is a sports writer for the Associated Press and has covered such events as the Super Bowl, Olympics, and World Cup. He lives in Garnerville, New York.

TABLE OF CONTENTS

GO, BILLS!

Buffalo, New York, is not a big city. Some people wondered if it would be a good place for a pro football team. The Bills' owner promised it would be a great place for a team. He was right. The Bills quickly became a strong and popular team. They won two championships in a row. Later, they played in the **Super Bowl** four years in a row. No other team has done this. Let's meet the Buffalo Bills.

Wide receiver Sammy Watkins (14) sprints away from an Oakland Raiders defender on December 21, 2014.

WHO ARE THE BILLS?

The Buffalo Bills are a team in the National Football League (NFL). They are one of the 32 teams in the NFL. The NFL includes the American Football Conference (AFC) and the National Football Conference (NFC). The winner of the AFC plays the winner of the NFC in the Super Bowl. The Bills play in the East Division of the AFC. They have never won a Super Bowl.

Defensive end Mario Williams takes down Carolina Panthers quarterback Cam Newton on September 15, 2013.

WHERE THEY CAME FROM

The Bills started in 1960 as one of the eight teams in the American Football League (AFL). In 1970, the AFL **merged** with the NFL. But the Bills' stadium was too small and old for the NFL. The team needed a new stadium, or they would have to move to another city. They got one. The new stadium opened in 1973, and the Bills stayed in Buffalo. The city is on the western edge of New York. The Bills are named after the legendary western settler "Buffalo" Bill Cody.

Running back Fred Jackson gets around a tackle in a game against the Kansas City Chiefs on November 9, 2014.

WHO THEY PLAY

The Bills play 16 games each season. With so few games, every one is important. Each year, they play two games against each of the other three teams in their division: the New York Jets, the New England Patriots, and the Miami Dolphins. The Dolphins and the Bills are big **rivals**. They have played each other at least two times every year since 1966.

The Bills offense gets set to run a play against the rival Miami Dolphins on November 14, 2014.

WHERE THEY PLAY

The Bills play in Ralph Wilson Stadium in Orchard Park, New York. The stadium is named after the owner who brought the team to Buffalo. After a recent update, it seats more than 72,000 people. Many people come from Canada to watch the Bills' home games because the stadium is close to the border. From 2008 to 2013, the Bills played one game per year in Toronto, Ontario. These were the first regular-season NFL games in Canada.

Ralph Wilson Stadium may not look big from the outside. But from the main entrance, the stands extend down to the field 50 feet (15 m) below.

HOME OF THE BUFFALO BILLS
RALPH WILSON
STADIUM
CHAMPIONS
1964
1965
CHAMPIONS
1990
1991
1992
1993
5
5
Ralph Wilson Stadium
Gate 5

THE FOOTBALL FIELD

HASH MARKS

END ZONE

20-YARD LINE

BENCH AREA

SIDELINE

GOAL POST →

MIDFIELD

GOAL LINE →

END LINE →

BIG DAYS

The Buffalo Bills have had some great moments in their history. Here are three of the greatest:

1964-65—The Bills won their first nine games in 1964. Then they beat the San Diego Chargers to win their first AFL championship. The next season, they again won the division and again beat the Chargers for the title.

1990—The Bills' fast-paced offense was almost unstoppable. They went 13-3 and beat the Los Angeles Raiders 51-3 for the AFC championship. They scored 428 points that season.

1992—The Bills went 11-5 in the 1992 season. They were losing to Houston 35-3 in a playoff game

Andre Reed (83) celebrates his third touchdown against the Houston Oilers in the 1993 playoffs.

on January 4, 1993. The Bills scored five straight **touchdowns** and won 41-38 in **overtime**. It is the largest comeback in NFL history.

TOUGH DAYS

Football is a hard game. Even the best teams have rough games and seasons. Here are some of the toughest times in Bills history:

1971—The Bills won only one of 14 games in their second NFL season. They gave up 394 points, 32 more than any other team. They scored only 184.

1985—Buffalo went 2-14. They were outscored 381-200. Coach Kay Stephenson was fired after four games.

1990-93—The Bills' greatest seasons in the NFL all ended painfully. They made it to four straight Super Bowls but never won the title. They lost to the Giants, Redskins, and twice to the Cowboys.

Running back Thurman Thomas (34) fumbles the ball in the Super Bowl on January 30, 1994. The Bills lost 39-13.

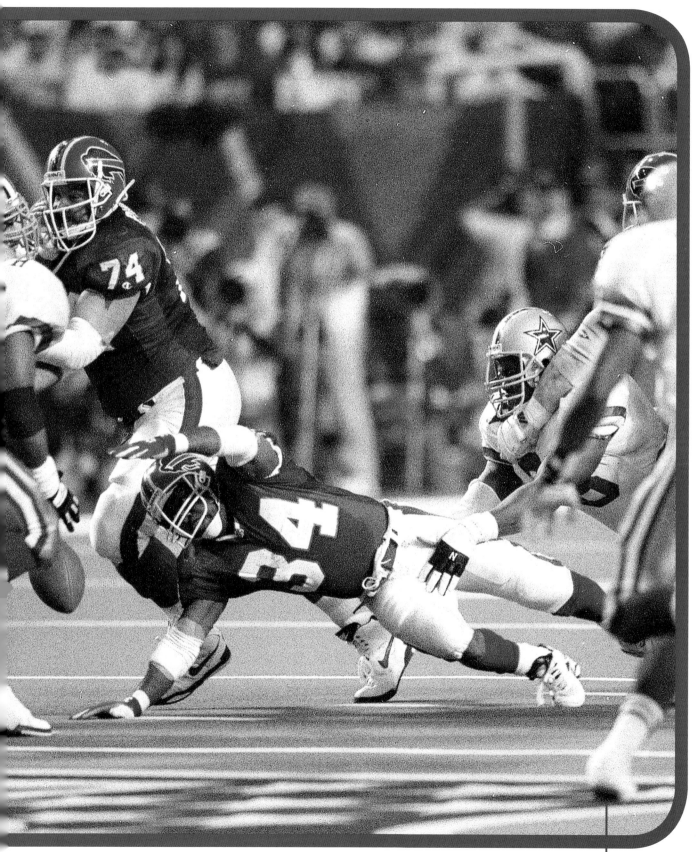

MEET THE FANS

The Bills' fans are known for being hardy. Buffalo is cold in the winter. But the fans turn out for every game. They **tailgate** outside the stadium then go inside and cheer loudly for their team. They have been known to help dig out one another's cars during snowstorms to get to games. The team's mascot is Billy Buffalo. Their cheerleaders are called the Buffalo Jills.

Bills fans celebrate a touchdown in a game against the Carolina Panthers.

HEROES THEN

Bruce Smith, Jim Kelly, and Thurman Thomas were the stars of the Super Bowl years. Smith was a threat to **sack** the quarterback on every passing play. Kelly was one of the best quarterbacks in the NFL. He was not afraid of taking a hit to make a play. Thomas was a great running back and receiver. All three players are in the Pro Football **Hall of Fame.**

In the AFL days, Jack Kemp was one of the league's best passers and leaders. Guard Billy Shaw did an outstanding job of protecting Kemp.

Jim Kelly (12) throws a short pass to fellow Hall of Famer Thurman Thomas (34) on December 30, 1995.

HEROES NOW

Bills receiver Sammy Watkins can energize the crowd at any time with a big play. The team added another playmaker in 2015. Star running back LeSean McCoy brings speed and strength to the Bills offense. On defense, the Bills have two star linemen. Mario Williams and Kyle Williams often sack the other team's quarterback. The Bills' owners are also heroes to Bills fans. Some fans worried the team might move to a different city. In 2014, new owners Terry and Kim Pegula promised to keep the team in Buffalo.

Mario Williams (94) and Kyle Williams team up for a sack against the Chicago Bears on September 7, 2014.

GEARING UP

NFL players wear team uniforms. They wear helmets and pads to keep them safe. Cleats help them make quick moves and run fast. Some players wear extra gear for protection.

THE FOOTBALL

NFL footballs are made of leather. Under the leather is a lining that fills with air to give the ball its shape. The leather has bumps, or "pebbles." These help players grip the ball. Laces help players control their throws. Footballs are also called "pigskins" because some of the first balls were made from pig bladders. Today they are made of leather from cows.

Bills receiver Sammy Watkins takes the ball into the end zone for an easy touchdown on October 26, 2014.

HELMET

SHOULDER PADS

GLOVES

THIGH PADS

FOOTBALL

CLEATS

SPORTS STATS

**H**ere are some of the all-time career records for the Buffalo Bills. All the stats are through the 2014 season.

RUSHING YARDS

Thurman Thomas 11,938

O.J. Simpson 10,183

RECEPTIONS

Andre Reed 941

Eric Moulds 675

PASSING YARDS

Jim Kelly 35,467

Joe Ferguson 27,590

INTERCEPTIONS

Butch Byrd 40

Tony Greene 37

TOTAL TOUCHDOWNS

Andre Reed 87

Thurman Thomas 87

POINTS

Steve Christie 1,011

Rian Lindell 980

Bruce Smith (78) had 200 sacks in his career, the most of any player in NFL history.

SACKS

Bruce Smith 171

Aaron Schobel 78

GLOSSARY

Hall of Fame a museum in Canton, Ohio, that honors the best players

merged when two groups join into one

overtime extra time that is played when teams are tied at the end of four quarters

rivals teams whose games bring out the greatest emotion between the players and the fans on both sides

sack when the quarterback is tackled behind the line of scrimmage before he can throw the ball

Super Bowl the championship game of the NFL, played between the winner of the AFC and the NFC

tailgate when fans gather outside of the stadium before a game to picnic around their vehicles

touchdowns plays in which the ball is held in the other team's end zone, resulting in six points

FIND OUT MORE

IN THE LIBRARY

Gilbert, Sara. *The Story of the Buffalo Bills.*
Mankato, MN: Creative Education, 2014.

Pitoniak, Scott. *Buffalo Bills Football Vault: The First
50 Seasons.* Florence, AL: Whitman, 2010.

Wyner, Zach. *Buffalo Bills.*
New York: AV2 by Weigl, 2014.

ON THE WEB

Visit our Web site for links about the Buffalo Bills:
childsworld.com/links

*Note to Parents, Teachers, and Librarians: We routinely verify our Web links to make
sure they are safe and active sites. So encourage your readers to check them out!*

INDEX